09/03 15.95

Discovering
South
America

URUGUAY

Discovering South America

URUGUAY

Charles J. Shields

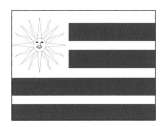

Mason Crest Publishers
Philadelphia

Produced by OTTN Publishing, Stockton, N.J.

Mason Crest Publishers
370 Reed Road
Broomall, PA 19008
www.masoncrest.com

First printing

1 3 5 7 9 8 6 4 2

Library of Congress Cataloging-in-Publication Data

Shields, Charles J., 1951-
 Uruguay / Charles J. Shields.
     p. cm. — (Discovering South America)
Summary: Presents information on the geography, history, economy, and people of
Uruguay. Includes a chronology, recipes, project ideas, and more.
Includes bibliographical references and index.
 ISBN 1-59084-290-1
1. Uruguay—Juvenile literature. [1. Uruguay.] I. Title. II. Series.
F2708.5 .S55 2003
989.5—dc21
                                                              2002011900

Discovering
South
America

Argentina		Paraguay
Bolivia	**South America:**	Peru
Brazil	**Facts & Figures**	Suriname
Chile	**Ecuador**	Uruguay
Colombia	**Guyana**	Venezuela

Table of Contents

Discovering South America

James D. Henderson

South America is a cornucopia of natural resources, a treasure house of ecological variety. It is also a continent of striking human diversity and geographic extremes. Yet in spite of that, most South Americans share a set of cultural similarities. Most of the continent's inhabitants are properly termed "Latin" Americans. This means that they speak a Romance language (one closely related to Latin), particularly Spanish or Portuguese. It means, too, that most practice Roman Catholicism and share the Mediterranean cultural patterns brought by the Spanish and Portuguese who settled the continent over five centuries ago.

Still, it is never hard to spot departures from these cultural norms. Bolivia, Peru, and Ecuador, for example, have significant Indian populations who speak their own languages and follow their own customs. In Paraguay the main Indian language, Guaraní, is accepted as official along with Spanish. Nor are all South Americans Catholics. Today Protestantism is making steady gains, while in Brazil many citizens practice African religions right along with Catholicism and Protestantism.

South America is a lightly populated continent, having just 6 percent of the world's people. It is also the world's most tropical continent, for a larger percentage of its land falls between the tropics of Cancer and Capricorn than is the case with any other continent. The world's driest desert is there, the Atacama in northern Chile, where no one has ever seen a drop of rain fall. And the world's wettest place is there too, the Chocó region of Colombia, along that country's border with Panama. There it rains almost every day. South America also has some of the world's highest mountains, the Andes,

Vacationers enjoy an afternoon on the beach in Punta del Este.

and its greatest river, the Amazon.

So welcome to South America! Through this colorfully illustrated series of books you will travel through 12 countries, from giant Brazil to small Suriname. On your way you will learn about the geography, the history, the economy, and the people of each one. Geared to the needs of teachers and students, each volume contains book and web sources for further study, a chronology, project and report ideas, and even recipes of tasty and easy-to-prepare dishes popular in the countries studied. Each volume describes the country's national holidays and the cities and towns where they are held. And each book is indexed.

You are embarking on a voyage of discovery that will take you to lands not so far away, but as interesting and exotic as any in the world.

(Opposite) Penguins wade into the surf at Punta del Este. Oil pollution along the coast of Uruguay is an environmental problem that kills hundreds of penguins each year. (Right) Montevideo, the capital of Uruguay, is known for its beaches, including fashionable Playa Pocitos, which is rimmed by high-rise buildings.

1 Land of Green Rolling Plains

URUGUAY, THE SMALLEST Spanish-speaking nation in South America, is about the size of the state of Washington. The Río Uruguay forms its western border with Argentina. Brazil lies to the north and east. The Atlantic Ocean and the Río de la Plata, an *estuary* of the Atlantic, border Uruguay in the south. Most of Uruguay is a green rolling plain, interrupted at two points by highlands of low hilly ridges. The narrow Atlantic coastal plain is sandy and marshy, occasionally broken by shallow lagoons.

Two Land Regions

Uruguay can be divided into two major land regions: the coastal plains and the interior lowlands.

The coastal plains curve along the Río Uruguay, the Río de la Plata, and the Atlantic Ocean. They cover about one-fifth of Uruguay. But most of the nation's population is concentrated in this region, especially along the southern coast. Montevideo, the largest city in Uruguay and its capital, lies on the coast near the point where the Río de la Plata and the Atlantic meet. Small family farms and large plantations occupy much of the western and southwestern coastal plains, which have Uruguay's richest and deepest soil. Beaches, sand dunes, and lagoons line the Atlantic shore.

The interior lowlands cover about 80 percent of Uruguay. Vast, grass-covered plains and hills and numerous rivers and streams make this area an ideal place for raising livestock. Sprawling ranches occupy most of the region, and small cities and towns dot the countryside. The Río Negro, the largest river in the interior, flows southwestward through the heart of the lowlands. A dam on the river forms Uruguay's only large lake, Lago Rincón del Bonete.

A long, narrow chain of highlands curves across the interior from the Brazilian border almost to the southern coast. Uruguayans call these highlands Cuchilla Grande (Big Knife) because knifelike formations of rock jut through the soil on many of the ridges. Overall, though, these hilly areas are remarkably featureless. The highest point in Uruguay, Cerro Catedral, rises 1,683 feet (514 meters) in the Cuchilla Grande.

A Water-Rich Land

Uruguay enjoys and abundance of water. Experts believe that in the language of the country's original inhabitants, "Uruguay" means "rivers of fishes." Large bodies of water bound Uruguay on the east, south, and west. Even the boundary with Brazil consists mostly of small rivers. Lakes and lagoons are numerous, and a high *water table* makes digging wells easy.

Three systems of rivers drain the land. Rivers flow westward to the Río Uruguay, eastward to the Atlantic and the tidal lagoons bordering the ocean, and south to the Río de la Plata. The longest and most important of the rivers draining westward is the Río Negro, which crosses the entire country from northeast to west before emptying into the Río Uruguay. But the Río Uruguay, which marks the border with Argentina, has low banks. During heavy rains, the river overflows, causing disastrous floods over enormous

A gaucho, or cowboy, guides a herd of cattle through green pastureland. Uruguay's low-lying grasslands are ideal for cattle ranching.

areas. A dam on the Río Negro at Paso de los Toros helps control the flow into the Río Uruguay. Behind the dam is a huge *reservoir*—Lago Rincón del Bonete. This reservoir is the largest artificial lake in South America. Flowing into the Río Negro is the Río Yi, its main *tributary*.

The rivers flowing east to the Atlantic are generally shallower, but their water level rises and falls more frequently. Many empty into lagoons in the coastal plain. The largest coastal lagoon, Laguna Merín (Lagoa Mirim in Brazil), forms part of the border with Brazil. A half-dozen smaller lagoons, some freshwater and some saltwater, line the coast farther south.

Cars ride down a street covered by ocean foam during a heavy winter windstorm in June 2001. High winds can be a problem in Uruguay, particularly in the winter when the pampero blows from Argentina. (Because of its location in the Southern Hemisphere, seasons in Uruguay are the opposite of those in the United States.)

Quick Facts: The Geography of Uruguay

Location: Southern South America, bordering the South Atlantic Ocean, between Argentina and Brazil

Area: (slightly smaller than the state of Washington)
total: 68,065 square miles (176,220 sq km)
land: 67,061 square miles (173,620 sq km)
water: 1,004 square miles (2,600 sq km)

Borders: Argentina, 360 miles (579 km); Brazil, 612 miles (985 km)

Climate: temperate, with damp springs and winters

Terrain: mostly rolling plains and low hills; fertile coastal lowland

Elevation extremes:
lowest point: Atlantic Ocean—0 feet
highest point: Cerro Catedral—1,683 feet (514 meters)

Natural hazards: seasonally high winds (the pampero is a chilly and occasional violent wind that blows north from the Argentine pampas), droughts, floods; with so few mountains to act as weather barriers, all locations are particularly vulnerable to rapid changes in weather fronts

Source: Adapted from CIA World Factbook 2002.

A Mild Climate

Uruguay lies in a *temperate* zone. It is the only Latin American country completely outside the Tropics. The climate is mild and generally the same through the country. Northwestern Uruguay, however, is farther from large bodies of water and therefore has warmer summers and milder and drier winters than the rest of the country.

In most of Uruguay, spring is usually damp, cool, and windy; summers are warm; autumns are mild; and winters are chilly and uncomfortably damp. High humidity, high winds, and fog are common. Winter warm spells can be abruptly broken by a strong *pampero*, a chilly and occasionally violent wind from the Argentine pampas (plains). There are no mountains to stop the wind's rush across the land. However, pleasant summer winds off the ocean can moderate warm daytime temperatures.

Rain falls evenly throughout the year. Amounts increase from southeast to northwest. Montevideo receives 37 inches (94 centimeters) annually, and the city of Artigas receives about 50 inches (127 cm) per year. As in most temperate climates, rain is the product of passing cold fronts. Thunderstorms occur frequently in the summer.

Environmentally Sensitive Wetlands

Much of Uruguay consists of rolling plains that are used for grazing sheep and cattle. But Uruguay's wetlands are special for a number of reasons.

Located on the Atlantic coast of Uruguay, the eastern wetlands contain fragile ecosystems. Butía palms, found nowhere else, grow in dense groves covering thousands of acres. Fields of tall grasses, floating grasses, rushes, and reeds support traditional Uruguayan crafts, especially basket weaving. Among the area's animals are a number of threatened or endangered species, such as the field deer, river wolf, straw cat, mountain lion, and dragon duck. River otters and carpinchos (large, semiaquatic rodents) roam the wetlands, too. More than 147 bird species, including many aquatic birds, breed here. Some live in the wetlands year-round; others are *migratory*. The warm, shallow waters are good places for fishing boats to find yellow clams, mussels, and shrimp.

Human activity has stressed the wetlands ecosystems. Hilly areas are used to raise livestock. Other parts of the wetlands have been converted to rice fields; rice farmers' dikes, ditches, and dams cut off the water flow, and their pesticides and fertilizers kill off insects. Tourism has spurred new highway construction, along with increased water pollution and soil breakdown. In the face of these pressures, the government of Uruguay is working with international agencies to find ways to protect its natural resources.

This steam locomotive has been working at the stone quarry at Paso de los Toros for more than 50 years. It carries stone for use as track ballast on Uruguay's government-owned railroads.

(Opposite) A cobbled street passes beneath an arched gateway in the city walls of Novo Colônia do Sacramento. This colonial settlement on the coast of Uruguay was established in 1680 by Portuguese adventurers from Brazil. (Right) Uruguay's president, Luis Batlle Berres, and his wife meet Argentina's Juan and Eva Perón on a boat in the middle of the Río de la Plata, 1948.

2 A Forward-Looking Nation

URUGUAY WAS A part of Spain's colonial empire in the Americas until the early 1800s. Then revolutionary forces drove out the Spanish. Brazil laid claim to Uruguayan territory until a peace treaty established Uruguay as an independent nation in 1828.

Throughout most of its history, Uruguay has enjoyed a democratic form of government, although bitter party rivalries caused much bloodshed in the 1800s and a *guerrilla* movement in the 1970s led to a harsh crackdown that resulted in more than a decade of military dictatorship. Democracy was restored in the 1980s. In 2001 and 2002, the financial troubles of its neighbors, Brazil and Argentina, adversely affected Uruguay's economy.

Early Settlement and Independence

Long before the arrival of European explorers in Uruguay, the Charrúa Indians hunted in the wetlands. They defended their territory fiercely. When the Spanish explorer Juan Díaz de Solís approached them by boat in 1516, they killed him and most of his men as soon as the Europeans landed on the riverbank. For the rest of the 16th century, the Charrúa turned away all outsiders. By the 17th century, though, the natives had begun trading with the Spanish.

For the next few centuries, the Portuguese and the Spanish competed to control trade on the Atlantic coast of South

The vertical line through the continent of South America on this 17th-century map marks the boundary established by the 1494 Treaty of Tordesillas. Spain was granted the land west of the line; Portugal, the land to the east, which the Portuguese eventually expanded into all of Brazil. Uruguay held a key strategic position between Spanish Argentina and Portuguese Brazil.

America. In 1680 the Portuguese built the settlement of Colônia do Sacramento (present-day Colonia, Uruguay) beside the Río de la Plata. A century earlier, on the opposite bank, the Spanish had permanently established Buenos Aires. In 1726, to counteract the threat of Portuguese expansion in the Banda Oriental area (the lands east of the Río Uruguay), the Spanish built a fort south of Colônia at Montevideo.

In 1776 this region was joined administratively with the territory of present-day Argentina in the Spanish *viceroyalty* of La Plata. Buenos Aires became the viceroyalty's major political and economic center, though it had some competition from Montevideo. Outside these coastal cities, *gauchos* (cowboys) herded cattle on the sparsely populated and virtually lawless plains.

In 1810 upper-class citizens of Buenos Aires rebelled against colonial rule, setting in motion the movement for independence that would eventually free all of Spain's South American possessions. The following year Uruguayan gaucho José Gervasio Artigas led a revolt against the Spanish at Montevideo. After several years of successes and setbacks, Artigas won control of the Banda Oriental. But the Portuguese in Brazil saw an opportunity to expand their territory. They overwhelmed the Uruguayans and in 1817 *annexed* the land.

Escaping to Paraguay, Artigas inspired those who would be later dubbed the "33 Immortals"—33 patriots who, under the leadership of Juan Antonio Lavalleja and with the support of Argentine allies, finally liberated Uruguay from Brazil in 1828. A peace treaty established Uruguay as an independent *buffer state* between Argentina and Brazil.

The Colorados Versus the Blancos

During the 19th century, two warring political parties split the loyalties of Uruguayans. The liberal Colorados wore red hatbands to distinguish themselves from the conservative Blancos, who wore white. Civil war broke out often as the two sides fought for control of the country, which opened the door to intervention from Uruguay's powerful neighbors, Brazil and Argentina. But when Paraguay entered the conflict by aligning itself with the Blancos, the Colorados united with Brazil and Argentina to fight against Paraguay in the War of the Triple Alliance (1865–1870). Although the Colorados and their allies won the war, both sides suffered heavy losses. Bitter fighting continued between the two rival parties until 1872, when they finally agreed to share leadership of Uruguay by alternating presidents.

Despite the conflicts, Uruguay prospered, thanks in large part to the involvement of Great Britain. British immigrants and investors introduced new wool, meat, and railroad industries. They also replaced poor-quality Spanish cattle with their own higher-quality breed. By the end of the 19th century, Uruguay had become a key supplier of beef, leather, and wool to the Western world. Immigrants from Europe, especially Italy, arrived by the tens of thousands looking for farmland and work.

In the early part of the 20th century, the Colorados elected José Batlle y Ordóñez to the presidency. He served two terms, from 1903 to 1907, and from 1911 to 1915. An unusually far-sighted leader, Batlle launched social programs that included medical and retirement plans, free education, laws protecting workers' rights, and public health reforms. But wealthy landowners blocked his attempts for fairer land-distribution policies.

During World War I in 1917, Uruguay broke off relations with Germany. Also that year, its constitution was amended to separate the church and the state. In 1920, when the victors of World War I formed the League of Nations—an international organization similar in some ways to the United Nations—Uruguay immediately joined.

Successes and Setbacks

Uruguayan democracy faced a setback in 1931 when the Blancos elected President Gabriel Terra, who demanded broader powers for the government. To stifle threats of revolt, Terra established a mild dictatorship with the help of his party. When the Colorado Party returned to power in 1938, a new

U.S. president George W. Bush meets Uruguay's president Jorge Batlle Ibáñez in the White House, February 2002. Batlle was visiting the United States to negotiate a free-trade agreement.

constitution was adopted that reversed Terra's policies and strengthened individual liberties. During World War II, Uruguay sided with the Allied cause and cut off relations with Germany, Italy, and Japan. It joined the United Nations when that organization was established in 1945.

During the 1960s, corruption in government eroded the country's prosperity. In 1967 an *urban* guerrilla movement, the Tupamaros, initiated a campaign of terroristic violence to overthrow the government. Four years later, the military took control of the government, dissolved Uruguay's congress, and hunted down Tupamaros as well as peaceful political opponents.

The military controlled Uruguay's political affairs until 1984, when Julio María Sanguinetti won the presidential election. Most Uruguayans were relieved when his government restored some democratic traditions and offered *amnesty* to political enemies. But there were no new policies established to help repair Uruguay's damaged economy.

In 1990 Luis Alberto Lacalle took office. Lacalle's plans to cut back on wages and reduce the government budget were necessary but unpopular. In 1994 Sanguinetti won a new term as president, serving until 1999. For his second term Sanguinetti emphasized Uruguay's participation in world trade markets. His successor, President Jorge Batlle Ibáñez, followed a similar agenda.

Economic progress was severely threatened in the first years of the 21st century. Argentina's economy collapsed and Brazil struggled under a huge debt burden, stifling Uruguay's prospects for growth. In addition, an outbreak of hoof-and-mouth disease among Uruguay's cattle compromised one of the country's major export products.

(Opposite) The state-owned La Teja oil refinery in Montevideo. Because Uruguay has no petroleum reserves, it must import all the oil it needs; as a result, the country's fuel prices are among the highest in Latin America. (Right) Fresh fruit is available at the Barrio Reus market. Agriculture is an important part of Uruguay's economy.

3 "The Switzerland of South America"

IN COMPARISON WITH many Latin American countries, Uruguay is fairly prosperous. The World Bank, an international development-assistance organization, estimated Uruguay's 2001 gross domestic product (GDP) per capita at $5,670. This placed Uruguay solidly within the ranks of middle-income nations worldwide. (GDP per capita, which measures each citizen's average share of a nation's annual economic activity, is similar to per capita income.)

A Livestock-Based Economy

The foundation of Uruguay's economy is four centuries old. In 1603, Spanish colonists released cattle and horses on the open plains of what is now Uruguay. The livestock thrived in the mild climate and vast natural pasturelands. By the early 1700s, there were millions of cattle in the region. Cattle raising, which had begun almost by accident, provided Uruguay with highly profitable exports—animal hides and finished leather. (Until refrigeration, meat itself could not be transported great distances.)

But over the next 150 years, the most rapid population growth happened in Montevideo, not the countryside. Prosperity attracted waves of job-seeking immigrants from the urban centers of Italy and Spain. Farm workers from Uruguay's *rural* areas migrated to Montevideo and other towns, drawn by the hope of better wages. Small industries, many owned by foreigners,

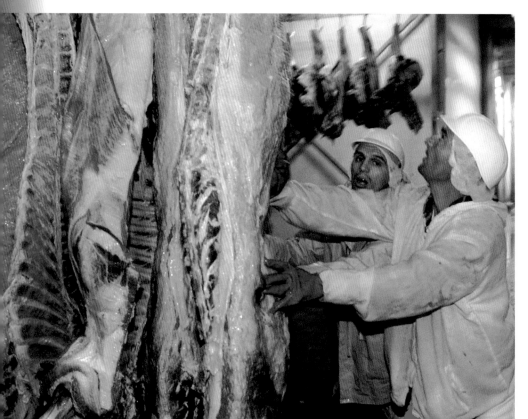

Workers at a packinghouse prepare meat to be exported in November 2001. Meat exports from Uruguay were suspended from April to November of that year because of an outbreak of hoof-and-mouth disease. Meat represents more than 20 percent of Uruguay's total exports.

needed workers to process the great quantity of agricultural goods arriving from the ranches and farms. Montevideo's workshops began turning out footwear, clothing, wine, tobacco, paper, and furniture.

"The Switzerland of South America"

By the early 20th century, Uruguay had achieved enough growth to earn the nickname "the Switzerland of South America." Livestock exports—mainly beef, mutton, and wool—and handmade goods noted for their craftsmanship created a high standard of living. Ambitious social welfare programs spread wealth throughout the society. In the first two decades of the 20th century, President José Batlle y Ordóñez launched radical social programs to improve education, labor conditions, and public health. Uruguay's middle class grew, and the country gained a reputation for social harmony.

But when export earnings dropped drastically during the Great Depression of the 1930s, Uruguay was hit hard. The government was forced to slash its social programs, and poverty became common, though not so widespread as in *Third World* countries.

The challenge for Uruguay's leaders over the last 40 years has been restore to prosperity. To a large extent, they have succeeded. In the middle to late 1990s, for example, Uruguay's GDP grew at an annual average of 5 percent. Unfortunately, the economic troubles in Argentina and Brazil—which combined account for about half of Uruguay's exports—took a toll. Uruguay's GDP declined by 1.3 percent in 2000 and 1.5 percent the following year. Still, analysts believed the Uruguayan economy remained fundamentally sound.

Uruguay's large middle class has been a key to its social stability. Only 6 percent of the nation's people live below the poverty line. (By comparison, the rate is about twice as high in the United States.) The country's workforce is also well educated. Almost all Uruguayan families own a radio, and there is about one television set for every four people. Uruguay has about two dozen daily newspapers. The largest are *El País* and *El Día* in Montevideo. Uruguay's constitution guarantees freedom of the press.

Good roads link all parts of Uruguay, but the country's railroad system, which is owned and operated by the government, is old and undependable. Most Uruguayans rely on the government-run bus system to go between cities and towns. A number of private companies also offer bus service.

Greatest Resource

Uruguay's most valuable natural resource is still its land. The country's grasslands provide excellent natural pasture for livestock. Uruguay's leading manufacturers process beef, hides, and wool. Montevideo serves as Uruguay's major ocean port.

Most of Uruguay's businesses and industries are privately owned, though the national government controls most utilities, much of the country's transportation industry, and some manufacturing firms.

Service industries account for 65 percent of Uruguay's GDP and employ 70 percent of the nation's workforce. Government agencies have the greatest number of service industry workers. Tourism, another leading employer, thrives along Uruguay's Atlantic coast. Many Uruguayans have jobs in hotels, restaurants, and stores at seaside resorts. Others are employed by

Quick Facts: The Economy of Uruguay

Gross domestic product (GDP*):
$18.43 billion
GDP per capita: $5,670
Inflation: 3.6%
Natural resources: arable land, hydropower, minor minerals, fisheries
Agriculture (6% of GDP): wheat, rice, barley, corn, sorghum, livestock, fish
Industry (29% of GDP): food processing, electrical machinery, transportation equipment, petroleum products, textiles, chemicals, beverages
Services (65% of GDP): government services, tourism, transportation

Foreign trade:
Exports—$2.24 billion: meat, rice, leather products, vehicles, dairy products, wool, electricity.
Imports—$2.9 billion: chemicals, machinery, metal goods, fuels.
Currency exchange rate: 26.47 Uruguayan pesos = U.S. $1 (November 2002)

* GDP = the total value of goods and services produced in a year.
All figures are 2001 estimates unless otherwise noted.
Sources: CIA World Factbook 2002; World Bank.

banks, health care facilities, schools, and firms in the transportation and communication fields.

Industry accounts for 29 percent of Uruguay's GDP and employs 16 percent of all workers. Meat packing and processing is the leading industry. Other manufactured goods include leather goods, *textiles*, beer, cement, and tires. Most of the nation's industrial plants lie in and around Montevideo.

Agriculture accounts for 6 percent of Uruguay's GDP and employs 14 percent of the nation's workers. Livestock raising is the leading source of

Members of Uruguay's bank workers' union, AEBU, gather in Montevideo's financial district in August 2002, to protest an order closing several banks. Financial troubles in Argentina and Brazil during 2001 and 2002 have had a negative effect on Uruguay's economy.

farm income. Cattle and sheep ranches occupy about four-fifths of Uruguay's total land area. Larger ranches may cover more than 5,000 acres.

Farmers raise crops such as corn, potatoes, sugar beets, sugarcane, and wheat in the fertile soil along the Río Uruguay and the Río de la Plata. Rice is grown in irrigated fields in the east. Most farms have modern mechanical equipment. But the poorest farmers use oxen-drawn plows and old-fashioned methods.

In the 1970s the government, seeing that the fishing industry could generate more revenue, offered aid to fishermen. Currently, a small government-supported fishing fleet catches anchovy, croaker, hake, and weakfish off Uruguay's Atlantic coast. Most of the catch is exported.

Uruguay has few mineral resources. Construction materials, such as gravel, sand, and stone, are the leading mineral products. Uruguay has no deposits of coal, petroleum, or natural gas, and thus must import large quantities of fuel. The country depends almost entirely on hydroelectric power for its electricity. Power plants on the Río Uruguay and the Río Negro supply electricity to all parts of the country.

Uruguay trades mainly with Western European nations, the United States, and its neighbors Argentina, Brazil, and Paraguay. These three South American nations and Uruguay are members of a trade federation called MERCOSUR. Uruguay's major imports include appliances, chemical products, machinery, metal goods, and various fuels. Beef, hides, live cattle and sheep, vegetable products, wool, and woolen textiles rank as the country's leading exports.

(Opposite) A colorfully costumed marcher plays cymbals on the streets of Montevideo during the Uruguayan Carnival celebration in February. (Right) A gaucho rides a wild horse at the El Prado rodeo, which each year draws gauchos from across the country to compete for the "best rider" trophy.

4 A Progressive People and Culture

SPAIN IS THE most prominent influence on Uruguay's people and culture. But in certain respects Uruguay differs from the other Spanish-speaking countries of South America. For example, the role of Roman Catholicism (and religion in general) is comparatively minor in Uruguay.

Makeup of the Population

Almost all of the original Amerindian inhabitants of what is now Uruguay were eventually killed by Spanish settlers or died of diseases brought by the Europeans. Today less than 1 percent of Uruguay's people claim Amerindian ancestry.

During the 1800s and early 1900s, large numbers of Spanish and Italian

Quick Facts: The People of Uruguay

Population: 3,386,575
Ethnic groups: white, 88%; mestizo, 8%; black, 4%; Amerindian, less than 1%
Age structure:
0–14 years: 24.4%
15–64 years: 62.6%
65 years and over: 13%
Population growth rate: 0.79%
Birth rate: 17.28 births/1,000 population
Death rate: 9 deaths/1,000 population
Infant mortality rate: 14.25 deaths/1,000 live births
Life expectancy at birth:
total population: 75.66 years
male: 72.32 years
female: 79.17 years

Total fertility rate: 2.35 children born per woman
Religions: Roman Catholic, 66%; Protestant, 2%; Jewish, 1%; nonprofessing or other, 31%
Languages: Spanish, Portunol, Brazilero (Portuguese-Spanish mix spoken on the Brazilian frontier)
Literacy rate (age 15 and older): 97.3% (1995 est.)

Source: CIA World Factbook 2002.
All figures are 2002 estimates unless otherwise noted.

migrant workers moved to Uruguay, joining the descendants of the original Spanish settlers. Today, most Uruguayans are descended from these immigrants.

Other groups with ancestral ties to Europe include people of English, French, German, and eastern European descent. About 4 percent of Uruguay's people are mestizos (people of mixed European and Indian ancestry). Less than 3 percent are blacks, whose ancestors were brought to Uruguay as slaves during the 1700s and early 1800s. Though one-quarter of the population claims Italian ancestry, Uruguayans speak Spanish and have built a cultural foundation on Spanish traditions.

Religion

The majority of the country is Roman Catholic, though surveys show that only a small percentage of Uruguayan Catholics attend Mass regularly. Unlike most other Latin American cultures, Uruguayans never wholly embraced the Catholic Church. The native Indians resisted being Christianized by Catholic missionary priests. In 1837 *civil marriage* was recognized, and in 1861 the state took over public cemeteries. In 1907 divorce (which was not recognized by the Catholic Church) was legalized, and in 1909 all religious instruction was banned from state schools. At the urging of President José Batlle y Ordóñez, complete separation of church and state was mandated in the new constitution ratified in 1917. Batlle went so far as to have religious holidays legally renamed. Today, for example, Uruguayans refer to Holy Week as "Tourism Week."

Uruguayan club soccer players battle for a ball during a 2001 match. Soccer is one of the most popular sports in Uruguay.

During the 20th century, Protestant sects began to grow in importance. Estimates in the late 1980s put the number of Protestants in Uruguay at about 2 percent of the population. From 1960 to 1985, the number of Protestants is estimated to have increased by 60 percent.

Jews make up a small proportion of the population (about 1 percent), with the majority living in Montevideo. The size of the Jewish community has dwindled since 1970, mainly due to emigration.

Social Conditions

Because of the social improvements that swept the country in the early 20th century, Uruguay has a high *literacy rate* and a large urban *middle class*. Income is spread fairly evenly—in other words, wealth is not concentrated in the hands of a small group of people, as is the case in many Latin American countries. The average Uruguayan's standard of living is

Uruguayan schoolchildren chat in the room where Uruguay's national assembly meets. The children were participating in a program in which they learned about the assembly and were able to ask their representatives questions.

better than that of most other Latin Americans.

Montevideo, with about 1.4 million inhabitants, is the country's only large city. The rest of the urban population lives in about 20 towns. During the past 20 years, an estimated 500,000 Uruguayans have emigrated, mainly to Argentina and Brazil. Because of Uruguay's low birthrate, high life expectancy, and high percentage of young people who emigrate, Uruguay's population is, on average, older than the populations of most countries.

Family Life

Changes in the law and national custom put Uruguayan women at a far greater advantage than other Latin American women beginning in the late 19th century. Civil, not church, marriage became legally required in 1885, and the influence of the Catholic Church declined. Divorce on the grounds of cruelty by the husband was legalized in 1907. In 1912 women were given the right to divorce if they had a specific cause. Married women were allowed to maintain separate bank accounts as early as 1919. These changes, coupled with access to free public education, opened the door to careers for women in Uruguay. In 1938 they voted for the first time.

By 1960 one-quarter of all Uruguayan women were in the workforce, finding help at home from the large number of housekeepers willing to cook, clean, and take care of children for modest wages. By 1975 one-fifth of all Uruguayan households were headed by women. Now, close to 60 percent of women work outside their home.

Middle-class Uruguayan families tend to be small—about 3.5 persons per household. Most women practice birth control. In rural areas, however, families tend to be larger and more unstable. Common-law marriages (unions with no legal contract) are widespread, as are instances of babies born out of wedlock.

Uruguay's educational system is excellent. Teaching is a respected profession and pays well. It is expected that girls will go to school and have careers. However, the schools in rural areas usually lack supplies, good classrooms, and better teachers.

Family gatherings in Uruguay often center on outdoor barbecues (*asados*). Another typical custom, symbolic of family and friendship ties, is the sharing of yerba maté, a form of green tea. A hollowed-out gourd (the maté), or sometimes a china cup, is packed almost full with green tea leaves. A metal straw is inserted into the tea, and boiling water is poured on top. The maté is then passed around in a circle, each person adding a little more hot water. Uruguayans drink gallons of maté every week.

Asados, parades, and other public celebrations often include folk music and dancing. Most of the country's musical and dance traditions (folk songs, polkas, waltzes) emerged from Europe, with the exception of the *candombe*, an African-influenced dance dating from colonial times.

Sports and recreation offer other occasions to bring families together. Amateur and professional soccer (called *fútbol* in Spanish) is very popular among the middle and lower classes. People of the upper classes generally prefer tennis, golf, and sailing. They usually try to escape Montevideo for the beach resorts on weekends and during the long summer holidays of December and January. For the rich, membership in a country club is a symbol of social status.

The city has expanded to such an extent that today its covers most of its department (a regional division similar to a county in the United States).The original area of settlement, known as the Old City, lies next to the port. But the central business district and the middle-class residential areas have moved eastward. The only exception is that banking and finance businesses continue to cluster in the Old City around the Stock Exchange, the Bank of Uruguay, and the Central Bank of Uruguay.

Today, Greater Montevideo is by far the most developed region of Uruguay and surpasses other regions economically and culturally. It is home

The Plaza Independencia, Montevideo, features the Palacio Salvo. At the time of its completion in 1928, the neo-Gothic structure was South America's tallest building, at 275 feet (84 meters).

to the country's two universities, its principal hospitals, and most of its communications media—television stations, radio stations, newspapers, and magazines.

Until a construction boom during the late 1970s, there were few modern buildings in Montevideo. In many parts of the city, elegant 19th-century houses built around a central patio are still commonplace. Some have large open-air patios. But most are covered by a glass roof that is sometimes made of colorful stained glass. Few of these houses are still owned by single families, however. Many have been turned into low-cost apartments.

The middle class of Montevideo tends to live in more modern apartments near the city center or the University of the Republic. Some choose a single-family *villa* with a small backyard. Many of these are close to the beaches running east from the downtown area along the avenue known as La Rambla, Montevideo's most important thoroughfare.

A beautiful metropolis, Montevideo offers extensive cultural activities and sightseeing opportunities. Attractions include the neoclassical Teatro Solís, which was completed in 1856 and named for the ill-fated Spanish explorer killed by natives in 1516.

The Plaza Independencia, a large square situated in the heart of the modern city, is lined by palm trees and dominated by a statue of José Gervasio Artigas, who is buried in the plaza. The neo-Gothic Palacio Salvo stands on the edge of the Plaza Independencia and marks the start of the Avenida 18 de Julio, Montevideo's premier shopping locale. Avenida 18 de Julio boasts a myriad of boutiques featuring the latest fashions and fine wool garments for all seasons.

Uruguay's 10 Largest Cities

		Population				Population
1	Montevideo	1,449,900	6	Tacuarembó		58,600
2	Salto	86,900	7	Artigas		52,500
3	Paysandú	76,400	8	Melo		52,200
4	Las Piedras	71,500	9	Treinta y Tres		46,200
5	Rivera	70,200	10	Mercedes		41,100

All figures are for 2002.

Rimming the Plaza Constitución, Montevideo's oldest square, are two historic buildings: the Cabildo (old town hall) and the Catedral Metropolitana (Metropolitan Cathedral). The ornate cathedral was completed in 1790.

The magnificent Palacio Legislativo took more than two decades to build; it has housed Uruguay's national legislature, the General Assembly, since 1925. The upper house, the Chamber of Senators, has 30 seats; the lower house, the Chamber of Representatives, has 99 seats. All legislators are elected to five-year terms by popular vote.

Among Montevideo's other attractions are many historic buildings, along with parks, plazas, and statuary. The city is also known as a good place to shop. Ceramic and leather goods are specialties.

Punta del Este

About an hour's drive east of Montevideo, in the coastal area of the country nicknamed "the Uruguayan Riviera," lies the fashionable resort

Small boats in the harbor at Punta del Este, a fashionable resort on the coast.

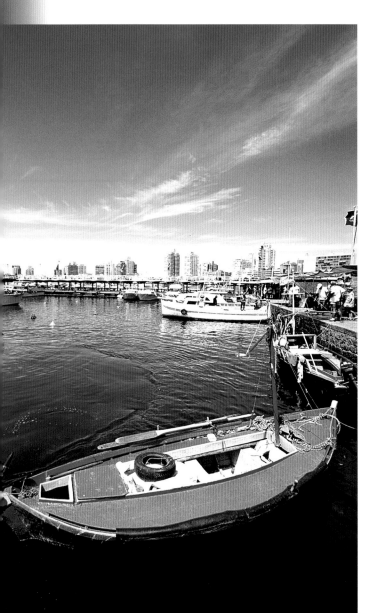

town of Punta del Este. One of the most popular vacation destinations in all of southern South America, the town attracts many well-to-do Brazilians, Argentines, and Uruguayans to its lovely beaches. Because it is located on a narrow peninsula, Punta del Este had to build up, and today it is blanketed by high-rise hotels, apartments, and condominiums that fill during the summer months with sun-loving travelers.

Other Towns and Cities

In addition to Punta del Este, the Uruguayan Riviera boasts dozens of beach resorts for vacationers. The old city of Maldonado, with its historic buildings, is also popular.

Salto (or Embalse de Salto Grande), founded about 1817, lies in northwestern Uruguay on the Río Uruguay, opposite the town of Concordia, Argentina. It is the second-largest city in the country and a road and rail hub. With a surrounding region that produces livestock, citrus fruit, sugarcane, grapes, and honey, Salto is a center for trade in grains and vegetables and also has a school of agriculture. Industries there include flour milling, meatpacking, shipbuilding, and the manufacture of chemicals, drugs, and wickerwork. Nearby are Salto Grande (the river falls) and the resort town of Arenitas Blancas.

Paysandú in western Uruguay is also located on the Río Uruguay. Founded in 1772, the city is a busy river port for oceangoing ships and has meatpacking plants, tanneries, and flour mills.

Las Piedras in southern Uruguay is near Montevideo. It is a rail and commercial center for a wine-growing and agricultural region. The gaucho nationalist leader José Gervasio Artigas scored a victory for Uruguayan independence over the Spanish here in 1811.

Rivera, in northern Uruguay, lies opposite the Brazilian city of Santana do Livramento, with which it shares a central street. The northernmost stopping point of the Uruguayan railroad system, Rivera is in an area producing fruits, livestock, tobacco, cotton, grains, and vegetables. It is also a cattle and sheep market. Textiles and tobacco products are manufactured in Rivera as well.

Melo, in northeastern Uruguay near the Brazil border, is an important regional transportation, manufacturing, and commercial center. The Spanish founded Melo in 1795 as a military post.

Mercedes, located in southwestern Uruguay, lies beside the Río Negro, near its mouth on the Río Uruguay. The city, which has road, rail, and air links to the capital, is a river port and trade center for the cattle, sheep, grains, and flax that are raised in the area. Industries include a prized wool market, grain processing, linseed-oil milling, and paper milling. A yachting center and health resort, the city also has a well-known musical society, an extensive rose garden, and parks along the river.

Festivals and Fiestas

Uruguay's most famous festival is the annual Carnival, which takes place on the Monday and Tuesday immediately preceding Ash Wednesday, the start of the Christian season of Lent. (Carnival may fall in February or March.) Most shops and businesses close for the entire week. Houses and streets are decorated, and comedy shows are staged at open-air theaters.

During the colonial period, black slaves used to perform their ancestral African dances and songs next to the fortified walls of Montevideo. White masters and their families would watch from the top of the walls on Sunday afternoons. When slavery was abolished, black Uruguayans continued their traditions, which, as time passed, maintained black folklore, the *candombe* and the distinctive drum rhythms accompanying it, and the carnival processions of performing groups. Las Llamadas, a special evening celebration carried out during Carnival, attracts thousands of tourists and local citizens. Dozens of bands representing different parts of Montevideo get together and perform. Local residents can tell where the musicians come from by the way they play.

In most Latin American countries, Holy Week—the week leading up to Easter Sunday—is a time of large public ceremonies linked to the Catholic faith. Because Uruguay maintains separation of church and state, however, Holy Week observances are generally confined to the insides of churches. In fact, coinciding with Holy Week each year are two secular (nonreligious) festivals: Tourism Week and La Semana Criolla (Creole Week), a popular celebration where the most outstanding riders in Uruguay and the neighboring countries come to show their skill. Spectators thrill to see bronco and bull riding, lasso tricks, and horse races.

Throughout the year, the Port Marquet neighborhood of Montevideo is a popular place to visit. This marketplace, constructed in the 19th century, is today a cheerful collection of barbecue restaurants. The streets are outdoor performance areas for musicians, jugglers, drummers, and watercolor artists.

Outside of Montevideo, old *estancias* (ranches) feature country food and folk shows throughout the year. In the towns, shops offer typical souvenirs such as *bombillas* (small tubes for drinking maté), *boleadoras* (hunting weapons used by gauchos), whips, harnesses, and saddles, as well as a variety of leather and wood crafts.

A Calendar of Uruguayan Festivals

Unlike most Latin American countries, Uruguay maintains a separation of church and state, both constitutionally and by tradition. This is reflected in the country's fiestas and festivals. Whereas important Roman Catholic feast days are occasions for public holidays or large festivals in other Latin American nations, in Uruguay this is generally not the case.

January

January 1, **New Year's Day**, is celebrated throughout Uruguay.

Uruguayans mark January 6, which in other Spanish-speaking Latin American countries is the religious holiday of Three Kings Day or Epiphany, as **Children's Day**. It is an occasion for gift-giving.

Also on January 6 is an important annual horse race similar in some respects to America's Kentucky Derby: the **José Pedro Ramírez Grand Horse Race**. Held at the Maroñas Racetrack, it attracts fans from all over Uruguay as well as Argentina and Brazil.

February

During **Carnival**, a two-day celebration preceding Ash Wednesday, Uruguayans hold parties and have parades featuring colorfully dressed marchers and musicians. (Carnival may also occur in March, depending when Easter falls in the given year.) **Las Llamadas**, a Carnival activity held at night, features performances by dozens of bands from throughout Montevideo; it attracts tens of thousands of tourists and locals.

March

Coinciding with **Semana Santa** (Holy Week) in Uruguay are the festivals of **Tourism Week** and **Creole Week**. The former features barbecues and folk music. The latter focuses on bronco and bull riding, horse races, and gaucho skills competitions.

Uruguay's Christians do celebrate **Easter** (which may fall in April in some years) by attending Mass and eating a large meal with family, but it is primarily a private matter, unlike Easter in other Latin American nations.

A Calendar of Uruguayan Festivals

May

May 1 in Uruguay is celebrated as **Día de los Trabajadores** (Workers Day).

The **Battle of Las Piedras**, a victory by José Gervasio Artigas, is commemorated on the sixth of the month.

June

June 19, the **Birthday of José Artigas**, is a national holiday.

July

Constitution Day is celebrated throughout Uruguay on July 18.

August

August 25 is **Independence Day**, marking the date in 1825 when Uruguayan rebels declared their freedom from Brazil.

October

October 12, **Columbus Day** or **Día de la Raza**, is a national holiday.

The 12th is also the day Uruguayans remember the important **Battle of Sarandí**.

November

On November 2, Uruguayans remember the dead. This is the **Día de los Muertos** (All Souls' Day).

December

The 25th of the month is **Christmas**, which Uruguayans typically celebrate with their families. In Uruguay the day is also called **Family Day**, a further reminder of the government's efforts to remove religion from public life.

Recipes

Celery and Pea Soup (*Sopa de Apio y Guisantes*)

(Serves 6)
1 head celery, chopped
6 cups vegetable stock
1 bay leaf
1 clove
6 tbsp corn oil
1 onion, chopped
1 clove garlic, chopped
6 carrots, scraped and chopped
1 tbsp all-purpose flour
1 lb tomatoes, peeled, seeded, and chopped
6 lbs young peas, defrosted, if frozen
Salt, freshly ground pepper

Directions:
1. Put celery into a large saucepan with the stock, bay leaf, and clove, bring to a simmer, cover, and simmer for 10 minutes. Set aside.
2. Remove the bay leaf and clove.
3. In a frying pan heat the oil and sauté the onion, garlic, bacon, and carrot until the vegetables are soft. Stir in the flour and cook for 1–2 minutes.
4. Add the tomatoes, stir and cook for 5 minutes.
5. Add all the cooked ingredients to the stock with the celery, cover and simmer for 5 minutes.
6. Remove the solids, place in a food processor, and reduce to a purée, then push through a sieve set over the saucepan.
7. Season to taste with salt and pepper. Cook the peas and simmer until they are tender, about 10 minutes.

Ambrosia

(Serves 4)
5 egg yolks
2 cups milk
1 tbsp cloves
Half a lemon, grated
1 cup sugar
1/2 cup water
1 tbsp vanilla

Directions:
1. Lightly beat 5 egg yolks and mix them with 2 cups of milk. Add gratings of lemon and cloves.
2. In another saucepan make a syrup with the sugar and water. Heat the water in a saucepan and mix in the sugar, stirring constantly until golden. Cool slightly.
3. Remove the syrup from the heat and pour into the mix of eggs and milk.
4. Put the mixture over the heat and cook it, stirring until clots appear and the liquid is concentrated.
5. Add vanilla and serve cold in bowls or cups.

Pascualina Pie

(Serves 8)
1 lb beets or spinach
1 onion, chopped
1 clove garlic, chopped
Pinch of grated nutmeg
Pinch of pepper
4 tbsp oil
3 tbsp grated Parmesan cheese
6 eggs
2 rounds of premade pie crust

Directions:
1. Preheat oven to 325°F.
2. Boil the spinach (or the beets, or a mix of both). Once cooked, drain well to remove all water. Mash the vegetables.
3. Brown the onion and garlic in the oil in a frying pan, and add the vegetables. Season with pepper and nutmeg. Set aside when the mixture is hot.
4. Cover the bottom of a pie dish with one round of pie crust. Pour the vegetables into the pie crust. Make five shallow holes in the vegetables to place the eggs (raw), like five points of a star, an inch or so away from the edge of the dish. Sprinkle Parmesan cheese over the top.
5. Cover the whole with the second pie crust and close, sealing firmly the edges.
6. Bake at 325° F as long as necessary for the crust to turn brown and flaky. When cut into slices, each piece will show the white and yellow of the eggs inside.

Stewed Lentils

(Serves 8)
1 lb lentils
6 cups water
3 medium carrots, sliced
1 onion, chopped
1 red pepper, chopped
1 tbsp (or cube) powdered vegetable broth
1 tbsp vinegar
Salt and pepper

Directions:
1. Sort the lentils and wash them.
2. Soak the lentils for 4–5 hours.
3. In a pot big enough to easily hold six cups of water, brown the onion and the sweet pepper.
4. Add the water, lentils, carrots, and powdered vegetable broth. Simmer covered for about two hours.
5. Once the lentils are tender, add the vinegar.

Glossary

adobe—a brick or building material of sun-dried earth and straw.

amnesty—pardon granted to a large group of individuals by the government.

annex—to incorporate territory (often seized by force) into a nation.

buffer state—a neutral state lying between two larger powers that are rivals of each other.

civil marriage—marriage conducted and recognized by the state.

estancia—a ranch.

estuary—a water passage where the ocean tide meets a river current.

gauchos—South American cowboys.

guerrilla—a person who battles a government or military using unconventional means such as sabotage.

literacy rate—the percentage of people who can read and write.

middle class—a class of people who are neither rich nor poor.

migratory—traveling seasonally to another place.

pampero—a strong, cold wind from the west or southwest that sweeps across the Argentine pampas.

reservoir—a human-made body of water used to conserve resources or create power.

rural—relating to the countryside.

temperate—in a warm, comfortable temperature range.

textiles—goods made with natural fibers.

Third World—term used to describe the poorest nations of the world; "developing nations" is synonymous.

tributary—a stream or river flowing into a larger body of water.

urban—relating to the city.

viceroyalty—an often large overseas territory governed on behalf of a monarch by an appointed official called a viceroy.

villa—a country estate or home belonging to a wealthy person, or a suburban residence resembling such a home.

water table—the upper limit of the ground soaked with underground water.

Project and Report Ideas

Travel Posters

Make a colorful travel poster advertising Uruguay as a place to visit. Use printed pictures from Internet travel sites to illustrate the poster.

Comparison Bar Graph

Create a bar graph showing the populations of the 10 largest cities in Uruguay and the 10 largest in the United States. Use two colors.

Exchange Student

Pretend that you were an exchange student in Uruguay last year, and make a scrapbook of your experience.

- Present to the class a picture of the flag (in color) from the country.
- Try to find an example of Uruguayan currency (major airport currency exchanges and some banks carry it). Find out what the exchange rate is between our country and Uruguay.
- Prepare a map and point out the city where you "lived." Be sure to pronounce the Spanish name correctly.
- Show some of the historic or popular places on the map that you visited with your imagined family. Why are they famous? Supply pictures.
- Play some music recordings from Uruguay.

Project and Report Ideas

Questions to Answer in a Paragraph

- What are the uses of a reservoir like Lake Rincón del Bonete in Uruguay?
- What are wetlands? (See Chapter 1.) Why are they important?
- Who were the Tupamaros? What did they demand?
- How is leather made?
- Who are gauchos?
- What happened to the Charrúa Indians?

Class Game

Divide the class in half. Have a contest to see who can spell the glossary words correctly, and then who can give correct definitions for each word. Finally, break into smaller teams and see which team can correctly use the greatest number of glossary words in a single sentence.

Chronology

1516 Charrúa Indians kill a party of Spanish soldiers led by explorer Juan Díaz de Solís. Their hostility discourages Spanish settlement.

1603 Spanish colonists release cattle and horses on the open plains of what is now Uruguay, then known as the Banda Oriental. The livestock thrive in the mild climate.

1680–83 The Portuguese and the Spanish compete to control trade in the Plata estuary.

1726 Montevideo, the future capital of Uruguay, is founded.

1811 José Gervasio Artigas leads soldiers to initiate a revolt against the Spanish forces vying for control of Montevideo and the rest of the Banda Oriental.

1828 Inspired by the brave revolts led by José Gervasio Artigas, Juan Antonio Lavalleja and his team of patriots, called the 33 Immortals, liberate the Banda Oriental from Brazil.

1865–70 Uruguay unites with Brazil and Argentina to fight against Paraguay in the War of the Triple Alliance.

1885 Civil marriages become legally required, replacing church marriages and further reducing the influence of the Roman Catholic Church.

Late 1800s–Early 1900s Large numbers of Spanish and Italian migrant workers immigrate to Uruguay.

1903–7, 1911–15 President José Batlle y Ordóñez launches social programs that include medical-aid and retirement plans, free education, laws protecting workers' rights, and public health reforms. The middle class expands and Uruguay gains a reputation for social harmony.

1920   Uruguay joins the League of Nations.

1931   Blanco Party elects Gabriel Terra, who demands stronger governmental control.

1938   Colorado Party returns to power; a renewed constitution strengthens individual liberties.

1967   The Tupamaros, an urban guerrilla movement, use violence to demand reforms.

1971   The military, citing the threat posed by the Tupamaros, takes control of the Uruguayan government and initiates a harsh crackdown on guerrillas and government critics.

1984   Julio María Sanguinetti is elected president, ending a long period of authoritarian rule.

2001–2   Brazil's economic problems, Argentina's political and economic crash, and an outbreak of hoof-and-mouth disease among Uruguay's cattle adversely affect Uruguay's economy; Uruguay leads a resolution sponsored by several Latin American countries calling upon Cuba to improve the political rights of its people.

Further Reading/Internet Resources

Bernhardson, Wayne. *Argentina, Uruguay and Paraguay.* Melbourne, Australia: Lonely Planet, 1999.

Bridal, Tessa. *The Tree of Red Stars*. Minneapolis, Minn.: Milkweed Editions, 1997.

Jermyn, Leslie. *Uruguay.* New York: Marshall Cavendish, 1999.

Morrison, Marion. *Uruguay.* New York: Children's Press, 1992.

Selby, Anna. *Argentina, Chile, Paraguay, Uruguay*. Austin, Tex.: Raintree Steck-Vaughn Publishers, 1999.

Travel Information

http://www.wtgonline.com/data/ury/ury.asp
http://www.mytravelguide.com/countries/uruguay/
http://www.lonelyplanet.com/destinations/south_america/uruguay/

History and Geography

http://www.countryreports.org/history/urughist.htm
http://www.encyclopedia.com/html/section/uruguay_history.asp
http://www.iexplore.com/dmap/Uruguay/History

Economic and Political Information

http://www.state.gov/r/pa/ei/bgn/2091.htm
http://www.countrywatch.com/cw_country.asp?vcountry=183
http://www.uruguayxxi.gub.uy/

Culture and Festivals

http://www.escapeartist.com/uruguay/art.htm
http://gosouthamerica.about.com/cs/urucult/
http://www.globalsources.com/tntlist/trvguide/uruguay/uru_bc.htm

For More Information

American Chamber of Commerce in Uruguay
Plaza Independencia 831, Oficina 209
Edificio Plaza Mayor
11100 Montevideo, Uruguay
(5982) 908-9186
amcham@zfm.com
http://www.zfm.com/amchamuru

The Embassy of Uruguay
1913 Eye Street, NW
Washington, D.C. 20006
(202) 331-1313/14/15
(202) 331-8142
uruguay@erols.com

U.S. Department of Commerce
Trade Information Center
International Trade Administration
14th and Constitution Ave., NW
Washington, DC 20230
800-USA-TRADE
http://www.ita.doc.gov

Index

Page
2:      © OTTN Publishing
3:      © OTTN Publishing
7:      Brand X Pictures
8:      Reuters NewMedia Inc./Corbis
9:      Bettmann/Corbis
11:     Stephanie Maze/Corbis
12:     Reuters NewMedia Inc./Corbis
15:     Colin Garratt; Milepost 92 1/2/Corbis
16:     Diego Lezama Orezzoli/Corbis
17:     Hulton/Archive/Getty Images
18–19: Digital Vision, Ltd.
22:     Manny Ceneta/Getty Images
24:     Jose Fuste Raga/Corbis

25:     Brand X Pictures
26:     Reuters NewMedia Inc./Corbis
30:     AFP/Corbis
32:     Reuters NewMedia Inc./Corbis
33:     Reuters NewMedia Inc./Corbis
35:     Reuters NewMedia Inc./Corbis
36:     Reuters NewMedia Inc./Corbis
39:     Reuters NewMedia Inc./Corbis
40:     Bettmann/Corbis
41:     Brand X Pictures
43:     Bettmann/Corbis
46:     Brand X Pictures

Cover photos: (front) AFP/Corbis; (back) Brand X Pictures

Contributors

Senior Consulting Editor **James D. Henderson** is professor of
international studies at Coastal Carolina University. He is the
author of *Conservative Thought in Twentieth Century Latin America:
The Ideals of Laureano Gómez* (1988; Spanish edition *Las ideas de
Laureano Gómez* published in 1985); *When Colombia Bled: A History
of the Violence in Tolima* (1985; Spanish edition *Cuando Colombia se
desangró, una historia de la Violencia en metrópoli y provincia*, 1984);
and coauthor of *A Reference Guide to Latin American History* (2000)
and *Ten Notable Women of Latin America* (1978).

Mr. Henderson earned a bachelor's degree in history from Centenary College of
Louisiana, and a master's degree in history from the University of Arizona. He then
spent three years in the Peace Corps, serving in Colombia, before earning his doctorate
in Latin American history in 1972 at Texas Christian University.

Charles J. Shields is the author of 30 books for young people. He has degrees in English
and history from the University of Illinois, Urbana-Champaign. Before turning to
writing full-time, he was chairman of the English and guidance departments at
Homewood-Flossmoor High School in Flossmoor, Illinois. He lives in Homewood, a
suburb of Chicago, with his wife, Guadalupe, a former elementary school principal and
now an educational consultant to the Chicago Public Schools.